# A Time of Change:

## Women in the Early Twentieth Century

### by Kristin Cashore

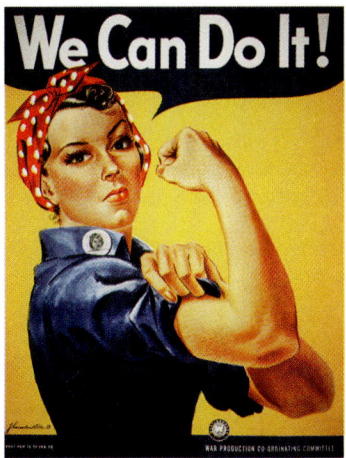

Editorial Offices: Glenview, Illinois • Parsippany, New Jersey • New York, New York
Sales Offices: Needham, Massachusetts • Duluth, Georgia • Glenview, Illinois
Coppell, Texas • Ontario, California • Mesa, Arizona

Every effort has been made to secure permission and provide appropriate credit for photographic material. The publisher deeply regrets any omission and pledges to correct errors called to its attention in subsequent editions.

Unless otherwise acknowledged, all photographs are the property of Scott Foresman, a division of Pearson Education.

Photo locators denoted as follows: Top (T), Center (C), Bottom (B), Left (L), Right (R), Background (Bkgd)

Cover: ©Bettmann/Corbis; 1 ©Corbis; 03 ©Jim Zuckerman/Corbis; 4 ©Bettmann/Corbis; 5 ©Schenectady Museum/Hall of Electrical History Foundation/Corbis; 6 ©Corbis; 7 ©MPI/Getty Images; 8 ©Hulton-Deutsch Collection/Corbis; 10 ©Corbis; 11 (T) ©Bettmann/Corbis, (CR) ©Corbis; 12 ©Hulton-Deutsch Collection/Corbis; 13 ©Corbis; 14 ©Corbis; 15 ©Marvin Koner/Corbis; 16 ©Bettmann/Corbis; 17 ©Bettmann/Corbis; 18 ©Underwood & Underwood/Corbis; 19 ©Bettmann/Corbis; 20 ©NASA/Roger Ressmeyer/Corbis; 21 ©Reuters/Corbis; 22 ©Jim Sugar/Corbis; 23 ©Jim Sugar/Corbis

ISBN: 0-328-13378-7

6 7 8 9 10 V0G1 14 13 12 11 10 09 08 07

## Introduction

Today in the United States, women have the opportunity to work at any job or profession they choose. No one thinks it is strange for a woman to be an athlete, police officer, or surgeon, or even run for President. But it wasn't always this way!

A hundred years ago, life was very different for women in the United States. They had fewer rights and many fewer career choices than men. Also, once a woman married, any property she owned became her husband's. Women were not even allowed to vote!

The early twentieth century was a hard time for many American women. But it was also an exciting time. It was a time of great change for women.

A hundred years ago, women could only dream of being firefighters. Today, many women are firefighters.

## Women's Roles in the Early 1900s

What was life like for women in the early 1900s? Most women worked at home. They cooked and cleaned. They took care of their children and husbands.

Men, on the other hand, earned the money, owned the family's property, and made most of the decisions.

Unmarried women had more freedom than married women. They could make contracts, sue in court, and own property. However, people looked down on them. Unmarried women were **criticized** for not being married.

Most women did not mind working at home. But some women felt **limited**. They wanted more control over their lives.

Then, in 1920, a new law was passed that gave women the right to vote. It was a sign of major changes to come.

# The Fight for Women's Rights

One of the rights women fought for was **suffrage**, or the right to vote. Women's suffrage did not happen overnight. The fight for suffrage took more than seventy years. One of the first leaders of the Women's Suffrage Movement was Elizabeth Cady Stanton.

In the early 1900s, most women took care of their homes, their children, and their husbands. Women did not usually have careers outside the home.

Elizabeth Cady Stanton was a housewife and mother. She was very unhappy with the state of women in the United States. She thought that women should be allowed to vote. She thought that women should be able to work at any job or in any profession they chose. She was unhappy that most colleges would not accept women as students.

On July 13, 1848, Elizabeth Cady Stanton met some friends for tea. They were in Seneca Falls, New York. Stanton's friends agreed with her about the need for rights for women. Over tea, they planned a **convention**, or meeting. The topic of the convention would be the rights of women.

The first Women's Rights Convention was held July 19–20, 1848.

Stanton wrote a "Declaration of Sentiments" for the convention. This declaration spelled out the unfair treatment of women. It also listed the rights she believed women should hold. Both men and women attended the convention. They agreed with Stanton's declaration. After the convention, Susan B. Anthony, Lucy Stone, and Sojourner Truth began to travel around the country giving speeches about the unjust treatment of women. Soon, women's suffrage became the major issue. If women had the right to vote, they believed, women could help bring about other reforms too.

Sojourner Truth escaped from slavery. She fought for women's rights, and for an end to slavery.

Giving speeches was not easy for these women. Men and women made fun of them. People shouted that they should be at home taking care of their families. Stanton and her friends got used to being criticized. They never gave up!

It was a long fight. As the years passed, more women joined the fight. Stanton's daughter, Harriot Stanton Blatch, and Stone's daughter, Alice Stone Blackwell, kept up the work of their mothers. In the early 1900s, Anna Howard Shaw and Carrie

Chapman Catt also worked for suffrage. They led a group called the National American Woman Suffrage Association.

When the Nineteenth Amendment was passed in 1920, women finally won the right to vote. It was a huge victory! The National American Woman Suffrage Association became the League of Women Voters. The group taught women about the importance of voting.

Of course, suffrage was only one step in the fight for women's rights. There was more to come!

Women marched, protested, and gave speeches in the fight for suffrage.

## Women in College

Even before the Women's Rights Movement began, new **opportunities** were beginning to open up for women. In 1833, Oberlin College in Ohio opened its doors to both men and women. It was the first college in the United States to do so.

Opening in 1839, Georgia Female College, now Wesleyan College, was the first all-women's college. Spelman, in Atlanta, Georgia, was the first college founded for African American women.

During the early 1900s, ideas about women were slowly changing. By the time women won suffrage, it was no longer unusual for women to enter college. By 1910, many women were even going to medical school.

In 1792, Sarah Pierce established Litchfield Female Academy in Litchfield, Connecticut. It was the first institution in America for the higher education of women.

By the early 1900s, it was not uncommon for a woman to go to medical school.

Of course, it was not easy for these women. There were still many men, and women, too, who thought that women should stay at home. There were people who did not think women were as smart as men. These people were **prejudiced**. Women knew that they were smart enough to do anything they chose to do!

In 1849, Elizabeth Blackwell graduated from the Medical Institution of Geneva in New York. She became the first woman doctor in the United States.

# Women in the Workforce

It was becoming easier for women to attend college. But it was not easier for women to get certain jobs. A woman might be hired as a secretary in a company, but probably not as a manager. Even women who went to college had a hard time getting some jobs.

Many women were school teachers, librarians, nurses, and secretaries. These were **accepted** roles for women in the 1930s. These were important jobs. The women in these jobs did important work. However, some women still felt limited. They wanted greater opportunities!

By the 1930s, few lawyers and judges were women. Most doctors were still men. Hardly any women were engineers or scientists. Many people were prejudiced against women who wanted to do "a man's job."

In the 1930s, most doctors were men and most nurses were women.

Of course, many women in the 1930s and 1940s were content to work only in the home as wives and mothers. But for those who dreamed of becoming business professionals, doctors, engineers, or lawyers, things were not promising.

We Can Do It!

WAR PRODUCTION CO-ORDINATING

War times created many opportunities for women. During World War II, some women served as nurses in the Army and Navy. Others took over the factory and office jobs of the men who went to war. Female reporters and photographers reported on the war. Some women even served as pilots! They did not fly in combat, but they flew as test pilots and in troop transport. When the war ended, however, these opportunities also ended. By the 1960s, however, women were gaining rights again.

Rosie the Riveter encouraged American women to show their strength and work for the war effort.

13

# Women in Government

In the early 1900s, it was very difficult for women to enter government service. Those who did were very strong and brave. They set the stage for today's female politicians.

In 1916, Jeannette Rankin of Montana was elected to the House of Representatives.

In 1922, Rebecca Felton of Georgia was the first woman appointed Senator. She was 87 years old at the time.

She was the first woman ever elected to the United States Congress. In 1924, Nellie Tayloe Ross of Wyoming became the first female governor in the United States. In 1932, Hattie Wyatt Caraway was elected to the United States Senate. Women's roles in government began to expand.

Jeannette Rankin was the first woman elected to the United States Congress.

Eleanor Roosevelt, the wife of President Franklin D. Roosevelt, was a very powerful woman. She worked tirelessly to help people all over the world.

In 1933, President Franklin D. Roosevelt chose Frances Perkins to be his Secretary of Labor. This was the first time a President named a woman to his cabinet. In 1945, Eleanor Roosevelt became a delegate to the United Nations. She used her power to help people in countries all over the world.

Still, today, most politicians are men. But this is changing. The day will soon be here when women hold as many government positions as men!

# Women Pioneers

**Pioneers** are brave people who do things that no one else has done before. In the early 1900s, there were many women pioneers. They did not care what prejudice they faced. They set goals, worked hard, and did amazing things!

Edith Wharton

In 1896, a piece of music called the *Gaelic Symphony* was played in the United States. It was written by H.H.A. Beach. It was the first symphony by a woman ever performed in the United States. In 1914, a woman named Mary Davenport-Engberg conducted an orchestra in the state of Washington. She was the first woman ever to conduct a symphony.

In 1921, Edith Wharton won the Pulitzer Prize for fiction for her novel, *The Age of Innocence*. The Pulitzer Prize is an award given every year to the best writers. No woman had ever won it before.

In 1926, Gertrude Ederle became the first woman to swim across the English Channel. To do this, she had to swim all the way from France to England! And she did it two hours faster than any man had done before! Ederle was only 19 years old. She became an instant hero. When she returned to her home in New York City, the city gave her a hero's parade.

When asked about her accomplishment, Ederle said, "People said women couldn't swim the channel, but I proved they could."

Gertrude Ederle braved cold, choppy waters to cross the English Channel. And she did it faster than any man had ever done it!

Amelia Earhart became the first woman to fly solo across the Atlantic Ocean. Her historic flight took place in 1932. In later years, she continued to break many records.

Amelia Earhart was a woman of the skies.

Also in the 1930s, Babe Didrikson Zaharias became one of the most famous athletes of her time. Babe, as everyone called her, was an amazing athlete. She was good at every sport she tried and there were many. At the 1932 Olympics, Babe won two gold medals and one silver in track and field. She ran the hurdles, threw the javelin, and jumped the high jump. In 1934, she became a golfer. She went on to win many golf championships. She was a true sports superstar!

The business world also had pioneers. In 1934, Lettie Pate Whitehead became the director of the Coca-Cola Company. No woman had ever been in charge of a major corporation before. This was a big first for women!

Another first for women was the All-American Girls Baseball League. During World War II, many male baseball players left to fight the war. Americans at home missed the game. So a new baseball league started, featuring women players. The league lasted from 1943 to 1954. During this time, many women became baseball stars. The league had many fans and gave a lot of talented women the chance to play in a sport that had kept them out.

Thanks to the brave pioneers who led the way, women were beginning to be all they could be!

Many thought of Babe Didrikson Zaharias as the "World's Greatest Female Athlete."

Today, women astronauts are pioneers of outer space.

## Conclusion

Today, American women work in every field imaginable! They are active in government. They attend the best colleges in the country and continue to break down barriers. And many women, college graduates or not, choose to stay at home to do another very important job—being a mother!

The changes for women over the last 150 years did not just happen. They were the results of the work of hundreds of thousands of women. These brave women spoke, marched, wrote, and organized. Women and young girls today must never forget the work of the women who have gone before them. They owe a lot to their "foremothers!"

Today, women are still fighting for equal rights. In some nations, the fight for women's rights has just begun. Today, the fight is not just for American women; it is for all women, everywhere.

We can learn from the brave American women who fought for women's rights in the 1800s and throughout the 1900s. If people around the world follow their example, life can improve for women everywhere!

"I think about how much we owe to the women who went before us—legions of women, some known but many more unknown. I applaud the bravery and resilience of those who helped all of us—you and me—to be here today."

—Ruth Bader Ginsberg, Justice of the United States Supreme Court

## Pioneers in the Classroom!

In the 1900s, some women chose unusual roles. For example, Gertrude Ederle chose to swim across the English Channel. Amelia Earhart chose to fly solo across the Atlantic Ocean. Babe Didrikson Zaharias became the world's greatest female athlete. Later, Sandra Day O'Connor became the first female Justice on the Supreme Court. Sally Ride became the first female astronaut in space.  And the list goes on and on.

Can you think of something you would like to try that you have never done before?  Brainstorm a list of first-time ideas with your classmates. The list might include ideas such as running for class president, putting on a play, raising money to help sick children, or cleaning up a park in your neighborhood. What is your idea?

1. First, meet with a small group of classmates and think about what you might like to do. Is it a job that you want to have when you grow up? Is it something you would like to do now? Is it something you would like to do in your home or your town? It's your decision!

2. Next, write your idea, or goal, on a piece of paper. Then, with your group, make a list of things that you will need to do to reach that goal.

3. Then, ask your teacher to set a time and a place for the group to meet. Assign a job to each person. Make a plan for each person to complete his or her job. What will you have to do first? next? last?

4. Finally, set a time and place to carry out your goal. Will you need help from your teacher to arrange a trip to the local park or for the use of the auditorium? Then just go for it!

# Glossary

**accepted** *adj.* regarded as right or correct.

**convention** *n.* a meeting of many people to discuss a topic.

**criticized** *v.* pointed out the faults of people or things.

**limited** *adj.* kept from certain roles; not allowed to do certain things.

**opportunities** *n.* chances to do something; possibilities.

**pioneers** *n.* people who are the first to do something.

**prejudiced** *adj.* having an unfair, hateful, and ignorant opinion about a person or group of people.

**suffrage** *n.* the right to vote.